Moment

with

God

for Single

Parents

PRAYERS FOR EVERY
SINGLE PARENT

RAMONA RICHARDS

DIMENSIONS
FOR LIVING

NASHVILLE

A MOMENT WITH GOD FOR SINGLE PARENTS

Copyright © 1999 by Dimensions for Living

All rights reserved.

No part of this work may be reproduced or transmitted in any form or by any means, electronic or mechanical, including photocopying and recording, or by any information storage or retrieval system, except as may be expressly permitted by the 1976 Copyright Act or in writing from the publisher. Requests for permission should be addressed to Dimensions for Living, P.O. Box 801, 201 Eighth Avenue South, Nashville TN 37202-0801.

This book is printed on recycled, acid-free, elemental-chlorine–free paper.

Library of Congress Cataloging in Publication Data

Richards, Ramona, 1957–
    A moment with God for single parents : prayers for every single parent / Ramona Richards.
        p.   cm.
    ISBN 0-687-97550-6 (alk. paper)
    1. Single parents—Prayer-books and devotions—English.
I. Title.
BV4596.S48R53   1999
242'.845—dc21   98-49919
                                                           CIP

Scripture quotations unless otherwise noted are from The New King James Version. Copyright © 1979, 1980, 1982, Thomas Nelson Inc., Publishers.

Scripture quotations noted NRSV are from the New Revised Standard Version Bible, copyright © 1989 by the Division of Christian Education of the National Council of the Churches of Christ in the United States of America, and are used by permission.

Scripture quotations noted NIV are taken from the HOLY BIBLE, NEW INTERNATIONAL VERSION®. Copyright © 1973, 1978, 1984 by the International Bible Society. Used by permission of Zondervan Bible Publishers.

Scripture quotations noted TLB are from *The Living Bible*, copyright © 1971 by Tyndale House Publishers, Wheaton, IL. Used by permission.

99 00 01 02 03 04 05 06 07 08 — 10 9 8 7 6 5 4 3 2 1

MANUFACTURED IN THE UNITED STATES OF AMERICA

CONTENTS

TRANSITION TIME

Be of good courage,
And He shall strengthen your heart,
All you who hope in the LORD.
—Psalm 31:24

Lord, thank you so much for my children. I realize that the time ahead of us will not always be easy—change never is. But there will also be laughter and good times. I know you will be with us, and I pray you will share your strength and wisdom with me during it all as we push our way through this time of transition— as we grieve and as we recover. Help us to always remember to find time to spend with one another.

THE RIGHT PUNISHMENT

"Then you will know that I am the LORD,
For they shall not be ashamed who wait
*   for Me. . . .*
I will contend with him who contends
*   with you,*
And I will save your children."
—*Isaiah 49:23, 25*

Let me remember you, O Lord, when I lose control of my emotions, and please forgive me for my anger. Help me deal calmly with my ex.

Visitation was this weekend, and my daughter waited. And waited. When she went back to her room, there were tears in her voice as well as her eyes as she blamed me, saying I shouldn't have been angry over the money.

Please give me the wisdom to convince my ex that there's a difference between punishing me and punishing our daughter.

And give her peace, especially when her parents act childish.

INFLUENTIAL FRIENDS
(A single mom)

I will pour My Spirit on your descendants,
And My blessing on your offspring.
                                    —Isaiah 44:3

Lord, please take care of my son and give him wisdom with his friends. And give me the knowledge to guide him without driving him away from us both.

I know how much he misses his father, and that he seeks some of that companionship in the company of older boys. But last night, he brought home a boy whose language and behavior could turn my son away from you. Please let it be the other way around. Protect my son and let him be the influential one. Let your light show through him.

I rely on you, who is Father to all children, young and old. Let him rely on you, too.

DISILLUSIONMENT

Let us not get tired of doing what is right, for after a while we will reap a harvest of blessing if we don't get discouraged and give up.
— *Galatians 6:9 TLB*

My personal belief in you, Lord of all, is not enough.

My daughter, who has watched me rely on you every day, has decided you don't exist. Her reasoning is flawless in her own teen-aged mind. How can there be a loving father in heaven when there isn't one here on earth? How can you be a provider when her own can't even remember her birthday? She refuses to see you in her life, so I ask you to help her see you in the lives of others. Help me show her that the magnitude of your love transcends anything we can know or imagine on earth. This is one task I cannot do alone. But I know you will be there to help us both.

JEHOVAH-JIREH

The LORD your God turned the curse into a blessing for you, because the LORD your God loves you. —Deuteronomy 23:5

God, thank you. Help me remember to praise you every day for your blessings and guidance. You are truly Jehovah-Jireh, the one who provides.

The two years since my divorce have been rough for all of us. Finances were tight and the clothes weren't always new, but we made it. I know the doors that opened—like the unexpected new job or the scholarship that let my oldest stay in college—were because you never forget those who love you.

Let me never forget that you love us, too.

FRIENDS FOR LIFE

A friend loves at all times.
—Proverbs 17:17

I want to praise you, Lord, for my friends. For friends who watch my children. Who don't try to set me up with that nice new choir member. Who don't act as if their children are better because Dad and Mom live in the same home.

Today, my next-door neighbor made me feel attractive without flirting and volunteered to watch my kids during that business dinner next week.

So I thank you for friends. And ask you to bless them as they have been a blessing to me.

FIRST DAY
(A single mom)

"I will be a Father to you,
And you shall be My sons and daughters,
Says the LORD Almighty."
                    —2 Corinthians 6:18

He looked so small, Lord, peering back at me, his eyes just above the bottom of the school bus window. They were brimming with unshed tears, belying the brave words he spoke at the bus stop. "It'll be fine, Mom. Dad will be proud of me."

I hugged him, blinking away my own tears. I hope that you will be proud of me, heavenly Father, that I didn't show the hurt his words caused. On a day that I wanted to be special for the two of us, he reminded me of his need for his father's approval. I try to understand. After all, I still seek your approval on my life.

AWESOME FIRSTS

Be of good courage,
And He shall strengthen your heart,
All you who hope in the LORD.
　　　　　　—Psalm 31:24

The trembling voice on the phone was ecstatic. "My first tooth!" she cried. "My first visit from the tooth fairy!"

Those awesome firsts of childhood! I've missed too many of my daughter's firsts because it wasn't my time to visit. She, or my ex, has always shared them later. But sometimes, "later" created as much ache as joy.

Lord, help her forgive my absences, and heal my own sense of regret. Instead, let me rejoice in her growth in this world as well as in your eyes.

BEYOND INJURY

Have I not commanded you? Be strong and courageous. Do not be terrified; do not be discouraged. —*Joshua 1:9 NIV*

Please forgive me, Lord, for my anger and my impatience. I should not have yelled when the call came two hours *after* my son's leg was set and casted.

But my fear was bile in my throat. Why did they wait, just because my name wasn't first on the insurance papers? Why does it always seem hard for people to make two phone calls when a child is sick or hurt?

Forgive me, and ease the pain my son is about to go through. Heal us both.

PRAYER SUPPORT

This is the confidence we have in approaching God: that if we ask anything according to his will, he hears us.
—1 John 5:14 NIV

Tonight, the leader of my Bible study group put my children and me on the prayer list. I felt honored and completely unworthy, and I was reminded once again of the unconditional love you have showered on your flawed and weak child.

I thought, too, of the many times that love was revealed through your church—the love they have shown and the support they have given as I traveled the rocky path toward being a single parent.

Thank you for giving us the spirit of your Son, wherever two or more are gathered.

THE ROLE MODEL NEXT DOOR

And we have known and believed the love that God has for us. God is love, and he who abides in love abides in God, and God in him. —1 John 4:16

The boys can't stop talking about him, Lord. Mr. K—who knows everything and does everything perfectly. And today they found out he coaches a baseball team, so his perfection is complete in their eyes. Now they want to go try out.

Lord, thank you for Mr. K and all the other adults who care about my children. They can't replace my sons' missing parent, but they—one by one—give them a better picture of unconditional love— and of you.

TO LISTEN AND HEAR

"I have called you friends, for all things that I heard from My Father I have made known to you." —*John 15:15*

Her eyes were intent as I prattled endlessly about my children and their escapades. She drank *two* cups of coffee before I stopped to take a breath.

When I asked for your help as I struggled to be a more balanced single parent, I did not know you would send that help in the eyes and ears of a friend. I had not realized how much I missed sharing with another adult, especially someone who knows and cares about my children. What a blessing she is!

Lord, I praise you for my friends. Thank you for their support, their patience—and, most of all, their understanding.

THE NEW MOTHER
(A single mom)

A merry heart does good, like medicine,
But a broken spirit dries the bones.
                              —Proverbs 17:22

Yesterday, my ex-husband and his fiancée picked up our kids. She's lovely and kind. They went to the park for ice cream, the arcade for games, and the movies.

Tonight my son informed me that she's more fun than I am. He said it was probably because she is a lot younger.

With him, I laughed. With you, I cry, because you know the intensity of the wound. Lord of all healing, cure my bitterness and show me the joy in this. Help me find a place for friendship with the woman who will be helping to raise my children.

LONELINESS AND SOLITUDE

And the peace of God, which transcends all understanding, will guard your hearts and your minds in Christ Jesus.
—Philippians 4:7 NIV

The difference between loneliness and solitude is a chasm as wide as the Grand Canyon.

In you, Lord, I find solitude and peace, which helps when the absence of my child leaves me with loneliness borne of jealousy and regret: jealousy that the home of my ex is filled with addictive warmth and family laughter; regret that the human promise of forever wasn't.

This time away is vital for my child. Help me find solitude in the midst of loneliness.

ADVICE
(A single mom)

The tongue of the wise promotes health.
The truthful lip shall be established forever.
—Proverbs 12:18, 19

She called me today, Lord. Wanting advice on raising my children—and on dealing with the quirks of my ex-husband.

Thank you, dear God, for giving me the strength not to laugh or get angry—and not to take advantage of her vulnerability. I was honest about the kids—although I reminded her that my advice about my ex would probably not be sound or levelheaded.

Watch over them, and guide her as her parenting skills are added to the mix.

POISON DARTS

Don't be impatient for the Lord to act! Keep traveling steadily along his pathway and in due season he will honor you with every blessing. —Psalm 37:34 TLB

Lord, I watch them across the room, and a dart pushes just a bit deeper into my heart. I'm jealous—of the way he fondly touches her arm, of the respect he shows her when he speaks to and about her, of the love he gives their children.

I know such jealousy is a sin that denies your timing and ability to work in my life. Please forgive me, my Lord who is always faithful. Give me the strength to rely on you to provide the emotional support I need when I need it. And let me rejoice in the happiness of my friends—not poison my own heart with envy.

FINDING THE TIME

Let all things be done decently and in order.
—1 Corinthians 14:40

Somehow, between the soccer game, band practice, that late meeting at the office, and deciphering the algebra homework, I forgot to make cookies for tomorrow's field trip. And no level of exhaustion could explain away the look on my six-year-old's face. So I'm making cookies while they sleep.

God, I am only one trying to do the work of two. Please help me prioritize my time more efficiently, saying "no" to the impossible and "yes" to the truly important. And help me remember cookies while the grocery store is still open.

FAITH'S IMPACT

But Jesus said, "Let the little children come to Me, and do not forbid them; for of such is the kingdom of heaven."
—*Matthew 19:14*

I watch my children play, and sometimes my concerns and cares for them bubble up around me like molten lava.

Mostly, I want them to know you, Lord of all creation. I want them to love and honor you, and feel the full impact you have on their lives. Am I doing all I can to achieve that? Do they see your light in me?

Guide me, dear God, as I seek to pass to them the faith of your salvation and provision.

A TEAM OF ONE

Correct your son, and he will give you rest;
Yes, he will give delight to your soul.
              —Proverbs 29:17

The words seem to burn through the teacher's note: "out of control."

We disciplined as a team, dear Lord. We stood together; now I stand alone against a son who doesn't understand divorce and a system that demands I play both disciplinarian and nurturer.

I desperately need your help: to correct as well as encourage, to be firm as well as loving. Let your strength back me as I tackle one of the world's hardest jobs—that of single parent.

A QUIET MANIPULATION

Fear the LORD and depart from evil.
It will be health to your flesh,
And strength to your bones.
                    —Proverbs 3:7-8

Perhaps it is because I am with our daughter every day that I saw quickly through her quiet manipulation of setting one parent against the other. And it would have worked, too, if the bitterness that separated my ex and me after the divorce still controlled us.

Thank you, Lord, for healing me of that, and for giving me the courage to make the first move. We may no longer be husband and wife, but through your grace and power, we can at least stand together as Mom and Dad.

THOUGHTLESS AND CRUEL

"Whenever you stand praying, forgive if you have anything against anyone; so that your Father in heaven may also forgive you your trespasses." —Mark 11:25 NRSV

Help me control my anger, O dear Lord, and curb my bitter tongue.

My son is lying on his bed staring at the ceiling, unwilling to say or do anything. Just staring. Apparently, my ex told him that he couldn't come over next weekend because they had an outing planned "just for the family."

It was a thoughtless and cruel thing to say. Give me the right words, Lord, to ease the pain, and help my son find a path to understanding. And I will need your strength to remain calm the next time I speak to my ex. I will not let this pass. My ex also needs to understand our son's pain.

A WISE DECISION

Yet in all these things we are more than conquerors through Him who loved us.
—*Romans 8:37*

I watched today as my son picked Cal for his ball team. It was a choice that probably cost him the game. When I complimented him, he just shrugged.

"Cal's fun," he said. "And it's just a game. You taught me that."

Lord, I know that pride is a sin, and I know that my son will make mistakes in his life ahead. But today was a day to praise him—and you—since one of the lessons I learned from my heavenly Father has successfully been passed to my earthly son.

THE OTHER SIDE OF THE FENCE

A sound heart is life to the body,
But envy is rottenness to the bones.
—Proverbs 14:30

The words of protest came through the phone like a plaintive wail.

"No," I insisted. "Come home now." I bit my lip to keep it from trembling.

My daughter's best friend lives only a block away, but their home is a different world. They have more kids, more dogs, more food, more toys—and two parents. And more than once, my daughter has turned a Friday night sleepover into a weekend getaway.

Heal my jealousy, Lord, and help me resist the temptation of trying to lure my daughter back with bigger and better "things." Show us the joy we have as a family, and help us rejoice in one another.

BRINGING HIM HOME
(A single mom)

*I will lead the blind by ways they have not
   known,
   along unfamiliar paths I will guide them;
I will turn the darkness into light before them
   and make the rough places smooth.
These are the things I will do;
   I will not forsake them.*
                    —Isaiah 42:16 NIV

He wants to meet my children—and he
shows no fear at all about this. I wish I
could say the same. I've been so careful,
Lord, to introduce only a special few to my
children. I didn't want them to meet a
confusing string of one-time dates.

What is the right time? Is there a specific
number of dates that entitles a man to meet
my children—or do I go only by how I feel?
Please share with me the wisdom of the right
words and the patience of proper timing.

ENDLESS STRENGTH

God is our refuge and strength,
A very present help in trouble.
Therefore we will not fear.
　　　　　—Psalm 46:1-2

When the fever broke at 104 degrees, it had been twenty-eight hours since my last nap. In two more hours, my other children will need lunches and good-bye hugs, and I'll have to call my boss and hope he understands about one more day off.

Exhaustion has a new definition for me today, Lord, and giving up completely sounds more than enticing. Every time I stand up, however, I feel your hand on my back, giving me just one more bit of strength. I simply could not do this without you. With you, I am never all alone, no matter how long the night.

Thank you.

SHARING TIME

To show partiality is not good,
Because for a piece of bread a man will
*   transgress.*   *—Proverbs 28:21*

There is just no sound quite like that of an aluminum bat making contact with a previously feared fastball. Although the pounding of my heart seemed almost as loud, as the ball sailed over the right-field fence.

His brother and sister are cheering now, even though they pouted and fussed over the nights they had to wait for supper or sit in the car while he finished in the batting cage. Learning that one parent can't always be split evenly into three pieces isn't an easy lesson. But their turn will come in time.

I pray, dear Lord, that you will help me make the wisest judgments when it comes to the important moments in their lives. Let none feel cheated—and all feel favored.

A MISSING COMPANIONSHIP

Lord, I have called daily upon You;
I have stretched out my hands to You.
—*Psalm 88:9*

The emptiness of my bed still haunts me, but it's not just the physical intimacy that I miss. I miss talking about my day with another adult, and taking pride and joy in what the children have accomplished. I feel odd telling my children about the trouble I had with my boss. They aren't ready for that kind of daily worry.

It seems strange to think of myself as lonely, when I have plenty of friends and two active children underfoot. But *lonely* is the only word I know that describes the sense that something vital is missing. So I turn to your Word for comfort, and I pray to you for patience. For I know that you, in your time, will find a human solution to my loneliness.

NIGHTTIME PEACE

And God is able to make all grace abound toward you, that you, always having all sufficiency in all things, have an abundance for every good work. —*2 Corinthians 9:8*

Late nights are the worst, Lord. The hours when the kids are asleep, and the house is completely quiet. My work is finished—well, almost—and my mind is still racing, processing the events of the day. That's when I'm overwhelmed with the sense that "I just can't do this alone. I *can't.*" There's too much to do, too much that one alone can mess up, too many things that could go wrong.

Thank you for your comforting presence during those times, God, with the reminder that, as my heavenly Father—and theirs—you are the best parent, the One who doesn't mess up. Help me pass this sense of comfort on to my children, even as I draw on it every day.

WRAPPED IN LOVE

I am persuaded that neither death nor life, nor angels nor principalities nor powers, nor things present nor things to come, nor height nor depth, nor any other created thing, shall be able to separate us from the love of God which is in Christ Jesus our Lord.

—Romans 8:38-39

I'm watching the snow fall tonight, Lord, and I feel a sense of peace and contentment I have not felt in a long time. The children are asleep, and as I sit next to the window with my hot chocolate, I just want to praise you and thank you for a day of small successes. No one got hurt, nothing important broke, the bills are paid, and most of the Christmas presents are wrapped and hidden. There aren't many, but every child has something special.

We all feel very loved. Thanks for sharing your love with me, God, so that one parent could love and share like a dozen.

THE REWARD IN LOGISTICS

Glory be to God who by his mighty power at work within us is able to do far more than we would ever dare to ask or even dream of.
—Ephesians 3:20 TLB

Logistics. That's a fancy word that means I have three kids, one ball practice, one band practice, one ballet lesson, one car, one parent, and forty miles in between. Supper sandwiches were grabbed at a gas station, and I dictated a memo to my boss with two bouncing in the backseat.

At home, three baths left a mire of towels, as I made lunches for tomorrow. Their beds doubled as trampolines until they heard my feet on the stairs; then there was a scramble for the blankets. Their attempts to look innocent made me laugh.

Thank you, Lord, for my children. And for my sense of logistics. Sometimes doing it all alone is its own reward.

FROM ONE PARENT
TO ANOTHER

Her children rise up and call her blessed.
—Proverbs 31:28

My mother called this morning, just to check in on me. She knew the kids were gone this weekend—"visitation rotation" as she calls it. Her voice was warm and cheering, and her words only a bit prying. Then, before she hung up, she said, "Just remember, I know where you've been and where you're headed."

I hung up, smiling. She has often reminded me that parenting is a tough job, single or not. But this time her words reminded me of you, Lord, and I think she knew it. She's the one who taught me that you know me inside and out—that you know where I've been and where I'm headed. So I'm calling on you, dear God, to help me teach my children as much about you as my mother taught me.

PRAYER AMONG THE SOAPSUDS

What happiness for those whose guilt has been forgiven! —*Psalm 32:1 TLB*

Today we washed the dog. I know it doesn't sound like a big event, but the kids turned it into a celebration of water and suds and joyous play. The dog wasn't the only one who was sprayed with the hose or slopped with a soapy rag. We had a glorious time—laughing and squealing and chasing each other.

And not once did they mention that this was my first time—that this was always something they did with my ex.

Thank you for dirty dogs, Lord. And for the love and forgiveness of children.

FALLOUT
(A single mom)

All your children shall be taught by the
  LORD,
And great shall be the peace of your
  children.   —Isaiah 54:13

My daughter's nightmares have deposited
her in my bed five nights this week. Each
time, she's snuggled close with the sleepy
words, "Don't leave me." Yesterday, I saw
my son hit a playmate hard enough to
draw blood. He is angry and unfocused.

No matter how we adults pretend
otherwise, our children do not go through
a divorce unscathed. I pray, Lord, that the
problems I see now are temporary. They
rely on us as we rely on you. Let them not
be disappointed yet again. As they develop
new routines and the upheaval around
them settles, help them find a new peace
and assurance.

EMOTIONAL BLACKMAIL

Keep your tongue from evil,
And your lips from speaking guile.
Depart from evil, and do good;
Seek peace, and pursue it.
The eyes of the LORD are on the righteous,
And His ears are open to their cry.
—Psalm 34:13-15

I hung up the phone, white and cold with anger. My son—*our* son—is graduating from kindergarten in a full ceremony— caps and gowns, diplomas, awards. And he will be receiving an award for his art. Naturally, he wants us both there.

My ex just said yes—but only if I'll give up next month's child support payment! I don't know what to do with my anger, Lord. How do I react to such emotional blackmail? Do I choose the importance of one evening over next month's budget? Do I return the guilt in kind? Help me, God, walk the right side of this fine line.

FEAR AND FRUSTRATION

Therefore humble yourselves under the mighty hand of God, that He may exalt you in due time, casting all your care upon Him, for He cares for you.
—1 Peter 5:6-7

Thank you, God, for letting that can of soup survive its sudden journey across the kitchen. I'm sorry the wall wasn't so fortunate.

And forgive me for my fear and frustration, Lord. Frustration at having too much to do and fear of what will happen if it doesn't all get done.

But I also want to thank you for the little reminders that you are always with me—like today. I threw the soup because the kitchen was still dirty. Then I heard my children laughing. I found them pawing through a sack of clothes a neighbor "just thought we might be able to use." It was a budget-saving thought. And a faithful one.

VISITATION RIGHTS

Your children like olive plants
All around your table.
Behold, thus shall the man be blessed
Who fears the LORD.
                              —Psalm 128:3b, 4

Every other weekend. Alternate Tuesdays and holidays.

Heavenly Father, it sounds like a gym schedule, not a time to spend with my children. I want to be there when they come home from school—when they lose a tooth, get a bad grade, or skin a knee. I don't want to play catch-up every other weekend as well as catch.

Help me avoid the trap of trying to use things to make up for my time away from them. Help me make the time I spend with them moments that are valuable to them because of who I am—a parent—and not just filled with what I can buy.

"WHY NOT?"
(A single dad)

My soul, wait silently for God alone,
For my expectation is from Him.
He only is my rock and my salvation.
        —Psalm 62:5-6

I tightened the last screw, then spun the wheel. The spokes sparkled in the sun as my four-year-old looked up at me in adoration. "You can fix anything!" she said brightly.

My ego soared. But only for a moment. Her mouth turned glum. "So why didn't you fix Mommy?"

How can I answer her question, Lord, when I don't understand the answers myself. Why didn't *you* fix her mommy? What will I say when she finally asks that one?

The "why" questions are the hardest, aren't they? Help me understand, and help me answer her questions calmly and carefully, even as I'm seeking the answers to my own.

BEING MOTHER AND FATHER
(A single dad)

Let patience have its perfect work, that you may be perfect and complete, lacking nothing.
—James 1:4

Tonight is the mother-daughter banquet at church. And this morning my daughter asked if I would take her anyway. "You're Mom *and* Dad," she said. "Why *can't* you go?"

I had no answer. How could I explain how painful church has become for me since her mother's death? Every family event, every message about family, causes what seems to be an unending ache. I can't imagine making it through that banquet intact.

I know I will heal. Until then, give me the strength to persevere and the wisdom of a mother as well as a father.

STARTING OVER
(A single dad)

The spirit of a man is the lamp of the LORD,
Searching all the inner depths of his heart.
—Proverbs 20:27

The words were shouted through a slammed door. "You're cheating on Mom!"

His sister's more rational words didn't help much. "Don't worry, Dad; he'll get over it in a year or two."

My date for the evening, who had heard it all, graciously offered to take a rain check on our date. She understands because she has two children of her own.

Lord, help me sort through the emotions—my own as well as my children's—as I start to date again. They are still hurting after their mother's death; don't let me dig that wound any deeper. Guide me with the dates I make—and the words I say to the people I love most.

KID'S CHOICE
(A single mom)

He who has begun a good work in you will complete it until the day of Jesus Christ.
—Philippians 1:6

Tomorrow, my son turns fourteen. Tonight, he's packing.

My ex has remarried, and they have a bigger house, with a pool. They live in a better neighborhood, with better schools. They have more money, with a convertible in the garage.

Tomorrow, they will have my son.

Lord, it's not an unwise choice on his part; I don't blame him at all. But I desperately need your help to deal with the change in my life and my lifestyle. How do I suddenly stop being a full-time mom? After my tears are dried, help me redirect my life in a way that changes this negative into a positive.

LIMITATIONS

Moreover it is required in stewards that one be found faithful.
                              —1 Corinthians 4:2

I am beginning to detest saying the word *no*. That may be because it's usually followed by the words, *But the other kids have . . .*

Tonight, my teen will help me do the monthly budget. I don't want him to have adult responsibilities yet, but he's more than old enough to understand the restrictions behind the words *single income*.

Please give us both the wisdom to understand and deal with our limitations and responsibilities toward each other—and you.

PURCHASING POWER

And He said to them, "When I sent you without money bag, sack, and sandals, did you lack anything?" So they said, "Nothing."
—Luke 22:35

When, dear God, did I teach my teenager that love equals purchasing power? Where did she learn that if I don't buy something she wants, then I must not love her?

Can you tell that the new "cool" school clothes are out? I started to ask you to help me teach her how to buy on a budget, but I think the problem goes deeper. I know that my ex sometimes gives her money when they're short on time, but I'm afraid I'm guilty, too.

Help me guide my daughter away from this attitude. Let her see in my life—my actions as well as my words—that money is not a substitute for love. No matter where or how she learned this, let the two of us change it now.

BRIGHT RIBBONS

*"There is hope in your future," says the
  LORD,
"That your children shall come back to their
  own border."*
                              —*Jeremiah 31:17*

Every day, my daughter takes one step
closer to being an adult—and I fight the
urge to keep her in pigtails and bright
ribbons.

Lord, I need your help daily as we walk
that fine line between teen and adult. Give
me the strength to let her go, and show
me how to pass to her the wisdom that
will let her make appropriate decisions
about her life.

May I always remember that she is
yours. Thank you for letting me raise her.

OF ALL THE GIRLS—

The way of a fool is right in his own eyes,
But he who heeds counsel is wise.
                                        —Proverbs 12:15

Lord, that girl is a wreck. Her hair is never combed, and her language consists mainly of words that can't be said on television. And if she's telling the truth about her experience with men, my son is in for a rough time.

He won't listen to me, and I'm not sure I'm the wisest voice for him to hear right now—I'm just a bit prejudiced. You, however, are omniscient. You know her heart—and his. Guide them. Let him be more of an influence on her than she is on him. And please give me the wisdom to know when—and what—to speak, and when to keep my mouth shut.

TEENAGE TRUST
(A single mom)

"Refrain your voice from weeping,
And your eyes from tears;
For your work shall be rewarded."
                    —*Jeremiah 31:16*

He seemed very nice. He spoke well, treated me with respect, and promised to have my daughter back by her curfew. So why was I pacing the floor earlier, trying not to blame her father for not being here? I was never a boy, but he was. He could better judge whether this young man was sincere.

Lord, thank you for nudging me down the hall where the pictures of her youth gather more memories than dust. I often used these to teach her about her heavenly Father as well as the earthly father she barely remembers. What a reminder that I've raised a cautious young woman who loves you and follows your ways. I did it by myself, but I was never alone. Nor will she be—tonight or in all her tomorrows.

FRIEND TO FRIEND

The LORD loves the righteous.
The LORD watches over the strangers;
He relieves the fatherless and widow;
But the way of the wicked He turns upside
*   down.*   —*Psalm 146:8b-9*

I listened without speaking, as her sobs slowly grew quieter. I sipped my coffee, knowing hers would go untouched. I had sat on her side of the table only a few years before, when coffee was the last thing on my mind. Her husband had made the announcement that morning. He was leaving. She could have the house, the kids, the cars. He just wanted out. She was still in shock.

How well I remember! Lord, please let my memories, my experiences give me the means to help her. Let her lean on me as well as on you as she works through the grief of her loss.

As you sent friends to me when I needed them most, let me be there for her.

HOLIDAY TREASURES

Behold, children are a heritage from the
   LORD.

—*Psalm 127:3*

As the holidays grow closer this year, Lord, help us rebuild our sense of family. We've become so scattered since the divorce, as if each of us were trying to survive alone. Let us draw on one another instead, rely on strengths, building up weaknesses, and bridging the gaps between us with new traditions and new ideas.

My children are priceless, and each has ideas of what would make the perfect Christmas or the perfect New Year's. Help me draw out the hidden treasures in my children as we celebrate the season of the ultimate gift—your Son.

THE ROD OF CORRECTION

Foolishness is bound up in the heart of
a child;
But the rod of correction will drive it far
from him. —*Proverbs 22:15*

Lord, please help me understand the difference between patience and a failure to discipline. The line gets much more blurred as my children get older and their language, music, clothes, and behavior become bolder and more challenging.

Parenthood is never a democracy, but I don't believe it should be a dictatorship either. Please give me the wisdom to let them test their limits without letting them get out of bounds. Let me see clearly when guidance should give way to correction.

Preparing them for life on their own is never easy, dear God. Help me as I teach them to fly.

LISTENING CLOSELY
(A single dad)

*Finally, all of you be of one mind, having
compassion for one another; love as brothers. . . .*
—*1 Peter 3:8*

Thank you, Lord, for stopping my words
tonight and opening my heart up to a friend.

The question was a stupid one, and I
almost pointed that out to him. "Do you
miss your children?" he asked.

Of course, I miss my kids! What kind of
father—? But I didn't say it. I felt your
nudge. So I said, "Why do you ask?"

Lord, let me be a brother to him as he
sorts through the problems in his marriage.
Give them the wisdom to seek counsel and
not make any final decision in haste or
anger. Let him see in me that being a single
father is never the easy answer, no matter
how good we are at the job.

UNEXPECTED HELP

I will lift up my eyes to the hills—
From whence comes my help?
My help comes from the LORD,
Who made heaven and earth.
—Psalm 121:1-2

Your help, Lord, sometimes comes from the most unexpected sources.

I started delivering the meals to shut-ins as a way to focus on others' struggles besides my own. Yet these devout men and women have taught me so much about you and about love—and about my own children. None was a single parent, but all struggled to raise faithful, healthy children, and all turned to you for help and guidance.

Thank you for the wisdom and memories of those who have walked this path ahead of me. Never let me doubt that you have always worked for the good of those who love you.

FIRST STEP
(A stepmother)

Be kindly affectionate to one another with brotherly love, in honor giving preference to one another.

—Romans 12:10

They look at me with wary eyes, trying to be defiant, not afraid.

"Why you?" they demand. Then they turn to their father. "You've dated others. Why her?"

Nothing since my divorce has been overwhelmingly easy, Lord, but this is more important than most of my struggles. Here are the hearts and souls of two children who are precious as well as precocious. I may not be their mother, but I do need to be more than just their friend.

Help us all understand one another, Lord. And let us remember to look to you for that help.

THE SAME PATH TWICE

But Jesus looked at them and said to them, "With men this is impossible, but with God all things are possible."
—Matthew 19:26

My children looked from one of us to the other. Finally, my son asked, "Are you sure you want to try this again?"

Excellent question. Just a glance over the past few years reveals more emotional and financial struggles than anyone should have to deal with. The past year, however, has been calm. As a family, we were finally on an even keel. Did I really want to change that?

Then I heard a soft voice beside me. "No one goes into this expecting to fail. We try, believing it will succeed and be better."

How true! Lord of all hope, please guide us as we cautiously but trustingly follow this path again.

A FLIGHT OF EAGLETS

Now may the Lord of peace Himself give you peace always in every way. The Lord be with you all. —2 Thessalonians 3:16

You would think, Lord, that all his weekends and holidays away would have prepared me for this. That, somehow, because I shared custody of my son with another household, I should be more ready for his final departure.

What a myth! The ratty used car he bought with his summer job money was overflowing this morning with his bedroom furniture and old dishes from our attic. This evening, it will park in front of an apartment building two hundred miles away. While his apartment is sputtering with activity and laughter, my house will crush me with emptiness and silence.

Your comfort, dear God, will be more important than ever as I deal with this new, unceasing loneliness.

THE CHILDREN OF OUR HEARTS

And the LORD *God said, "It is not good that man should be alone."* —Genesis 2:18

I do not envy my daughter and her fiancé their task, and I ask, Lord, that you give them guidance in their choices.

"This is the one!" she announced to me over the phone. "Can we come this weekend?"

And what a weekend it will be for them! Her parents are divorced and remarried. So are his. Four announcements with a long list of complications. Who gets told first? Who gets told last? Do they tell her parents in a different way than they tell his? Already their lives are filled with emotional stumbling blocks, and they aren't even married yet. Help them, and us, remember that this is *their* moment. Help us put aside unreasonable expectations and honor and cherish the children of our hearts.

AND TWO SHALL BE ONE

Therefore a man shall leave his father and mother and be joined to his wife, and they shall become one flesh. —Genesis 2:24

Thank you, dear God, for my healing, and for that of my ex. Only you made it possible for us to put aside the vast chasm between us long enough to celebrate this day with our children.

For today is a celebration for the bride and groom, not for two whose past and present hurts cloud the rest of their world. Today, these two pick up where we left off—joining together as one in a promise of forever. This is your perfect picture of love in this world, and only you can make the promise survive. Let our children remember that, as we come together to celebrate their future.

SINGLE GRANDPARENT

And patience develops strength of character in us and helps us trust God more each time we use it until finally our hope and faith are strong and steady.

—Romans 5:4 TLB

And we thought negotiations for visitation times would stop when our children were grown.

What a beauty this child is, Lord! She already has a major hold on my heart, and I would gladly and eagerly spend time each day with her. But this grandchild of divorce not only has two parents, she has *seven* grandparents, each as devoted as I am. So, even as I see the humor in all of us scrambling for time to adore her, I'm asking you for a new kind of patience—a patience of waiting and a tolerance for the ideas and rights of other grandparents. Be with us all as we enter this new dance in our lives.

ROLE MODEL

The Spirit Himself bears witness with our spirit that we are children of God.
—*Romans 8:16*

I know that my children love and cherish me, Lord, but please don't let them hold me up as the model parent. I made too many mistakes—the first one being a divorce. There are much better models for them as they build their marriages and their families.

I do love them, and I tried to teach them about the depth of your unconditional love. That's a good foundation, but show them how to build above and beyond that through your entire family and through your Word. Help them see that you are the only perfect parent.

AFTER ALL IS SAID AND DONE

Your sun shall no longer go down,
Nor shall your moon withdraw itself;
For the LORD will be your everlasting light,
And the days of your mourning shall be
*   ended.*

—Isaiah 60:20

Thank you, O dearest Lord, for answered prayers. Thank you for the wisdom and patience you gave me when my children were young. What a wonderful gift you bestowed on me when you left these wonderful lives in my charge! I will be eternally grateful to you for every time you guided my hand or gave me the proper words.

Now that they are grown, let me be a friend and mentor as well as a parent. Let me continue to show them your light in my everyday life, so that they will always know—as I did—I was a single parent, but I was never alone.